From the Res
of
Resilience

Candace S. Shepherd

DEDICATION

I dedicate this book to all the beautiful beings on a continuous journey to learning, loving and being their authentic selves. To the lost, confused, depressed, insecure and broken - there is always a chance for evolution. I wish for this book to assist you on the road to recovery.
To the over-extenders and over lovers, this is a reminder that you are important too; deserving of being loved just the way you love others, so take time to love on yourself and never leave yourself out. My final dedication goes to myself - this is the first piece of published work that is a manifestation of the internal work I desire to share with others.

ACKNOWLEDGEMENTS

I would like to thank Hiwot Adane for her commitment to reviewing this book and editing it thoroughly. My appreciation to Chelsea Allamby and Felicia Guy- Lynch for providing their genuine feedback and suggestions contributing to making this work the final masterpiece it has come to be.

Additionally, gratitude to Dre Donovan who did an amazing job at transmuting my vision of the book cover into a beautiful design I adore.

CONTENTS

My desire to write this book arose from the need to share the tools I have acquired with beings alike; those who are on their personal journeys and may need reminders to stay on the track of progression. On my very own journey of loving and knowing myself, I have observed that confidence and high self-esteem is vital in maintaining love and trust for ones' self. I have experienced various difficult situations and often felt as if I had nowhere or no one to turn to so I learned to turn inward. I have had to motivate and push myself to do what I would consider the right thing, according to my values and principles, and found that you can be your own worse critic or greatest cheerleader.

There were times throughout my life where I had to alter my self-talk as I understood, I was only hindering myself. Instead, I modified it to positive self-talk by digging deep within me and pulling out the false ideas I held about myself as well as the outer world. In a world that can sometimes be cold, great guidance can make a huge difference. The most beautiful thing is that change is always possible and an inevitable process.

As writers of our own stories, we choose whether our everyday decisions will grant positive outcomes or negative ones. We learn that there are experiences in life that are impossible to control as situations may seem like they appear out of nowhere. However, we fail to realize that our true power lies in how we choose to deal with these situations; it is also this same notion that shapes the events to follow.

As I mentioned earlier, making smart decisions and doing what's best begins with us having confidence in ourselves and thinking highly of yourself. If you believe you are capable of achieving something, you will be able to. Adversely, if you believe you are unable to accomplish something, you will also not accomplish it. It literally begins with our thoughts, our thoughts then become actions.

Having a low regard for yourself can come from experiencing abuse or observing abuse, having been neglected as a child, not being nurtured by elders with positive speech or words of affirmations. Childhood trauma can breed insecurity, if you were put down or beaten whether physically, emotionally or mentally, you may begin to believe that you are not able to be better than what the abuser programmed you to believe.

There are various reasons why one can become insecure. When I was younger, I was less confident than I am now because I was scared to speak up for fear of not being accepted or praised especially from my parents. I was the type of child who did what they were supposed to do so that I could be considered good and that carried on until early high school, I obeyed, and I attained good grades. It was in my early teenage years where I realized that I needed to stand up for what I considered was right and not remain quiet especially when it came to abuse or injustice just for the sake of being accepted even if it was to family.

When things are not sitting right in your spirit, that is an indication that it is going against your morale, against your core principles and values, against your wisdom. We can not let our past or unhealthy childhoods consume us and turn us into toxic human beings. We have to step up to the challenge and make continuous choices to heal our pain, heal our trauma and take steps to move on to the good that truly serves, or we will hurt others and perpetuate the cycle of abuse even if it is on a subconscious level. Part of that is owning our shit and where we are not taking accountability for our own lives.

This book hopes to share affirmations, poems, quotes and reminders with you in hopes that some of them if not all will resonate, teach, inspire or move you. They are personal, mental tools that I have used in my evolution to become the self-assertive, resilient, confident person that I am today. I hope the words filled in this book can fill you and assist you in being introspective and proactive on your own journey as well as allowing you to connect with myself and my ongoing journey. There is always another person out there that can relate to you even when you feel alone and like no one understands. Everything may not resonate with you as various messages are for various people at various points in their lives. I am hopeful that at least one message will touch you and that alone is a blessing.

Remember, you are your greatest possession, treat yourself accordingly.

Peace and Love to you. Enjoy.

1 LOVE AND LOSS

Love is not a battle, I will not fight you nor force you to love me wholeheartedly.

There is no harm in detachment to achieve a greater good. Release yourself from the guilt of letting go or removing yourself from a person or situation who does not align with your higher self (best self).

Are you settling in any area of your life? (Write down the reasons why you are settling below and then evaluate and assess whether they are valid reasons or excuses and fears you are projecting that keep you away from attaining your true desires?

_____

_____

_____

_____

_____

_____

_____

_____

_____

_____

_____

_____

_____

_____

_____

_____

_____

_____

_____

_____

Write any steps you can take to improve your life that would counteract the settling you have written down on the previous page.

_____

_____

_____

_____

_____

_____

_____

_____

_____

_____

_____

_____

_____

_____

_____

_____

_____

_____

_____

_____

_____

_____

_____

One of the worst mistakes you can make is waiting on someone to change.

You deserve you the most. Full Stop.

The Company I Keep

I don't have to be in company with someone for an extended period or "know" them to see through them. Energy speaks. I read through people. I read energy and actions. I hold the gift of discernment.

I am very selective with whom I associate and befriend. If someone is fraudulent, a liar, dishonest, deceptive, fake, they will be cut loose.

Friend is a valued title that I hold near and dear, not just anyone gets the privilege of receiving it.

A friend is someone who has my best interests at heart.
A friend does not seek to covet from me, deceive me, manipulate me or be jealous.

A friend of everybody is a friend to nobody.

If you think someone's intentions are just what they voice to you, you're naïve.

Take no one at face value.

Get right or get left.

Innocence/niceness is at times the greatest guise for deceit and disingenuousness.

They say keep your friends close and your enemies closer, I don't want any enemies close to me.

Show me who you are so I can throw you in the trash or on the contrast, place you up on my mantle piece.
Many may be able to fool the world but you can't fool me. Who are you really? Take off your masks, reveal yourself as I don't have the patience for the pleasantries that get us nowhere.

And just when I thought we were on the same page, we were on the same page number of two completely different books.

A lack of knowledge regarding what a healthy relationship entails is to your detriment.

Love alone (acceptance of one's totality) is not enough to keep a relationship thriving. You need other ingredients such as: respect, transparency, openness to grow, understanding, reciprocity, alignment of values, tolerance and commitment for a healthy relationship. With love alone, a relationship will fail.

Love is easy, it's boundless. Respect requires more effort. People are quick to love but falter with giving respect and valuing others especially when they do not value nor respect themselves or their own bodies.

Discern, Discern, Discern…

Love, but do not leave logic behind.

If someone wants to screw themselves over by not appreciating your greatness, let them. The Karma of losing you will be by far all that is needed to hurt them and in the same vessel, teach them a valuable lesson.

If they can and will repeatedly lie to you about small things
then they can and will lie to you about big things.

If you stay where you're not supposed to, you'll never receive what is really for you.

Loving or having strong feelings for someone does not equate to that person being a great life partner for you or even a great life-long friend.

No, a person should not change for the person they love, a person should change for themselves first and the by-product of that change can satisfy the person they love.

Don't lose your king or queen focusing on your lust for the pawns. The pawns are sacrificial.

We tend to shun or criticize others when we don't understand them. A lack of understanding can be the difference between rejection and acceptance.

Can't have you how I want you so I don't want you at all…I refuse to barter with my heart.

Compromising yourself is compromising your sanity. Certain situations require adjustments but not of your core values and principles. If you compromise enough, you won't even be able to recognize yourself anymore.

Relationships; Attachment Is Nice but Respect Is
Paramount.

Desperation only leads to difficulties. Don't be desperate for love or acceptance, desire it but be patient in your quest for it.

Love is accepting someone in their totality irrespective of their flaws, mistakes and short comings. Love is separate from attachment and we can still love those we choose to detach or seek space from.

Love is an energy, separating ourselves from someone in the name of healing, progressing, protection of self, attaining happiness and/or peace does not mean that there was no love. True love is not possessive, it's freeing it knows no bonds. The choice to have a relationship or the state of a relationship or partnership is separate from the energy of love or loving someone.

Transparency

Please forgive me if I seem a little reluctant for I did not expect such a glorious gift so soon…

You see, I know I had asked God many times for a love so divine that it would seem fictitious but I never imagined that it would arrive so soon…

This love has swept me off of my feet, forced me to break down my walls and to open the gates to my heart once again.

This love has brought visuals of us being forever to the frontal lobes of my brain.

Your energy is like a drug that sedates me…it is like a thick smoke that engulfs me but I do not want to escape…. even with the awareness that it could suffocate me, I would gladly surrender to my death.

Your love feels like the sun glistening on my back as I bathe in the seas of Barbados…warm and inviting.

You taste like the sweetest thing that I've ever known, you are like a kiss on my collar bone.

You embody the essence of freshness.

Your embrace allows me to feel safe and secure, a comfort that is newly found but has an intrinsic familiarity.

And although it feels so right, I have allowed doubt and reluctance to seep into my mind, past failed relationships and standards unfulfilled by unequipped souls have tarnished my innocence and vulnerability.

Brazenly, I am pushing that aside in the name of love, in the name of freedom, in the name of friendship, in the name of the spirit, in the name of stability, in the name of passion, in the name of serenity.

Positivity begets positivity so today I am being positive, I am positive that our love can endure a lifetime.

Nothing is a coincidence and neither was the day we met for our paths were already chosen for us and it was written in the scripts of our lives that we should be together some day and change the lives of one another for an eternity.

When I look at you, I see a mirror.

Our love is enriched with one of the most important tools in a long-lasting union. Transparency.

Partners who don't pull their share of the weight are too costly.

Ex is an ex for a reason, experience for what you never
want to experience again. Moving on.

I Never Lost my Faith

I grew up middle class
My childhood was all fun and games
But the happiness didn't last

Nine years old standing before the man who planted his
seed in my mother to create me
I called him father
Strong in my stance as I stood in the way

My dad had just chased my mother with a knife,
What a twisted circumstance,
I stood there dumbfounded as I asked myself, "Could this
be life?"
What came afterwards was nothing short of strife

The police were called, it was the first time I saw a man cry
and the only time I had seen my father cry,
Handcuffed and imprisoned, it was nothing short of a
temporary goodbye

Restraining order, court battles, fear
Separation…the tears

But through it all….I never lost my faith

Fast-Forward, I kept it moving, head up and being an
Earth Sign, my feet grounded
Doing well in school, but seeking unnecessary company to
fill a void, I wasn't prepared for what was to come in the
next few years

Sixteen, pregnant and afraid, I told him he could leave but he stayed…
Truth is, maybe it would've been better if he had gone…

I was young, naïve and vulnerable
Opening my legs and letting him get too comfortable
Unlike myself, I soon found out love wasn't in his customs though

But one thing I know is….I never lost my faith

First, came the deception, cheating, mood swings, he could've resembled a chameleon
Then came the control, living within boundaries, I almost lost my soul
But I never lost my faith….

My last straw was the abuse, how could you disrespect the mother of your child?
It was logically impossible for a valid conclusion to be deduced.
I produced…..this lovely prince

Broken glass, holes in walls, laptops smashed, aggressive calls.

But I never lost my faith…

Looked within myself and knew I had to leave; it was hard to believe and conceive…
That I became the product of an abusive cycle….
The stress, depressed, none the less, the memories were repressed

How could a queen like me fall victim to such ill-treatment,
I ended the relationship and immediately felt relief

I witnessed my father abuse my mother, saw it destroy my
brother, I couldn't let it happen to another

Could no longer live in denial, this perpetrator passed his
place, but now I am reborn and it's because the Universe
knows…that I never lost my faith

2 SELF REFLECTION: MIRROR MIRROR

Accountability is the first step towards change, the first step towards help, the first step towards healing and the first step towards growth.

Doubt and fear will keep you captive and hold you stagnant forever as long as you allow it to.

Don't play the victim when you're also the perpetrator.

Practicing self-love and being true to you is not about deceiving and betraying others.

Anger is a beast you have to tame by overpowering it with logic and patience.

Speak with your energy and actions. You don't need to convince people of who you are, your behaviours and practices will paint the picture.

The most important love is the love you nourish yourself with. Be self-prioritized. Prioritize yourself but do not become solely fixated on self that you completely neglect caring about others.

If you see a problem with the world in general, fix it in the capacity you know how to, even if it is on a micro/personal level. Be what the world needs. Small ripples still have an effect.

If you don't like who you are, change it. Be who you want to be. You're not limited. Seek knowledge to grow and evolve.

What you say you are and present yourself as is not who you are. Who you are is your thoughts, actions, behaviours, character and sprit that is active even when no one is watching.

You can be your own worst enemy or greatest accomplice. You choose. Speak life into yourself regularly, your body and mind are your essential vehicles in this physical world. Our spirits spend a lifetime connected to or within them, make the best that you can out of the experience. You have the power to nourish your mind and body with fruits and seeds of thought that will birth power and motivate action from the inside, outwardly.

It's quite okay to be quiet or reserved. It is not okay if you are not able to assert yourself when matters demand that you do. People will manipulate and control you when you don't speak up for yourself. Don't worry about rubbing people the wrong way, worry about your dissatisfaction, unhappiness and mental instability as a result of not asserting yourself.

Don't let people walk all over you, you're not a "welcome" mat.

When you're being selfless and everyone is being selfish,
where does that leave you?

Starve your ego and feed your spirit. There is power and evolution in taking responsibility for your wrongs and your impact in affecting someone else's life negatively. Right your wrongs. Take accountability for your behaviours.

The simplest yet the hardest thing we can do to make the world better is make ourselves a better being.

People learn by example. Heal your traumas, seek help, work on yourself, take accountability for your actions or lack thereof, forgive yourself, be the change you want to see, be the love that you desire. Be a light in places of darkness by making conscious, deliberate choices to do so.

Careful not to succumb to what's easy because greatness takes work. Don't succumb to your lower self because growth demands discomfort. We'll never be perfect but we can always seek to be better versions of ourselves than we were yesterday. Unpack all of the weight that you need not carry forward with you in your evolution.

Be what you are looking for. Give to yourself what you
seek from others. Reflect what you require.

It's your job to heal your insecurities, not your partners or anyone else's. A partner can definitely choose to aid or offer you support on your journey.

However, it is ultimately up to you to decide whether certain habits or patterns of behavior are problematic or not, to address and confront them head on, be aware of where they are stemming from and to make a conscious effort starve them of power if you are to evolve from them.

Being a healer to and for others does not absolve you from
the responsibility of having to heal your self. It's loving and
essential at times to take a break from tending to others to
heal and serve ourselves.

You don't give a chance for others to accept you completely when you are not being yourself. Be not who you think society wants you to be but who you are at your core as long as it's not harmful to others. Being an abuser is one of those things that is not justifiable to me as a natural way of being. Aside from that, the more we pretend to be who we are not, the more we grow away from loving, knowing ourselves, healing and evolving.

We operate from our own level of understanding. If we want to elevate that, we have to be open to being receptive to other understandings. Our own understandings are not the only truths that live.

You will never understand something until you make the conscious choice to be open to understanding it or receiving understanding from it.

We will never be perfect but we can always strive to be better than we were before, better versions of ourselves. And "better" is what better means to you, there is no set formula. Define your own better. Be your own Boss.

Stillness can be beneficial, being stagnant is not. For even when you're still or making little progress, you can be moving forward mentally and emotionally in preparation for the physical work ahead. Wholly trinity; mind, body and soul. Get yourself right. Being progressive in one of the areas, does not negate the necessary work to be done in the other areas.

Extreme pleasure seeking and over-indulgence are forms of escapism. Observe yourself, check yourself, taking anything to the extreme can be problematic. Balance is key.

What are your ways of distracting yourself from a painful, stressful memory, situation or experience?

_____

_____

_____

_____

_____

Do you think your modes of distraction are healthy or problematic?

_____

_____

_____

_____

_____

If you do find them problematic, what are you going to do about it?

_____

_____

_____

_____

_____

We do not have to fall victim to any of our naturally adapted tendencies or defense mechanisms. Unlearn to learn.

Stare in the mirror naked, bare, every day until you fall in love with your reflection.

Starve your insecurities and feed yourself with acceptance, focus on your best features and what you love about yourself.

What you don't love, if it can be changed through discipline, diet and exercise, start working on it, one day at a time.

As for what you don't like, analyze why you don't like it and whether you have held on to false belief in regards to what should be considered attractive and unattractive.

Learn to be attracted to yourself. Get comfortable with yourself and body by staring at it. Touch it regularly, be free.

Your guilt can be your greatest guide. It directs you towards how you can be better by showing you the areas in which you have dissatisfied or disappointed yourself..

3 BUILDING, BRICK BY BRICK

Trying and doing poorly is better than having never tried at all. You can always grant yourself yet another chance at improving your previous attempt. Something is better than nothing. Do it.

Please protect my soul from demons, evil and lost souls
attracted to me in hopes of feeding off of my energy and
resources (If there is a spiritual energy, entity, a god or gods
you believe in, this is to be repeated to them).

And even if it takes an eternity, I will wait for the love that was created for me.

I'm not perfect but I'm progressive.

I seek to change no one. Change in someone's character may manifest merely by my presence or involvement in their life. Leading by example is a form of teaching, we can't force feed change down the throats of those who are unwilling, not ready or who simply do not desire to.

It's not about what you like, it's about what you deserve.

Keep asking yourself "why" until you get to the root of your problem and confront it. Be conscious of why you do the things you do, make the unconscious, conscious. Being the dark to light in order to heal it. You can not heal that which is hidden and you are unwilling to face.

I am powerful.
I am capable.
I am strong.
I am wise.
I am the creator of my own reality.
I am the painter for my canvas.
I can accomplish anything that I set my mind to.
I am not limited by the beliefs other project on to me.
I am not what others say I am.
I am who I know I am.
I am learning.
I am growing.
I am a beautiful work in progress.
I forgive myself.
I love myself.

Make sure you're preparing yourself and are ready for what you're hoping and praying for because if not, you can easily sabotage it once you get it.

Being led by fear will lead you astray. The very thing you try to avoid, you will attract. If you're scared to be open about who you are, your past, your setbacks, flaws and entirety with someone because you think they won't accept you or will abandon you, you won't get the acceptance you crave since the person doesn't know the real you.

Accept yourself first and that not everyone is meant for you.

If you are transparent and someone walked away because of it, it doesn't mean you should never be transparent again with others. It could serve as an indication for self-reflection and growth and as a confirmation that the person you shared with was not meant to stay in your life. You two were not to be acquainted for the long term. Having love for someone does not equate to the promise of forever. Release the fear, let go of holding on tightly and hiding all that is you.

Your life will improve, once you reflect sincerity, you will begin to attract sincerity.

I will commit to loving myself wholeheartedly.
I will prioritize my mental health and sanity.
I will protect myself from harm by making healthy,
conscious decisions that are in my best interest.
I will put myself first.
I will set boundaries so that others can not take advantage
of me or coerce me into going against my will.
I will create personal values and uphold them.
I will have faith in myself.
I will trust myself.
I will nurture myself.
I will teach myself.
I will be myself unapologetically.
I will free myself.
I will overcome all of my struggles and setbacks.

Count your blessings. What we may overlook and consider little things daily are usually big things. We don't realize how valuable "little things" are at times until they are taken away. Practicing gratitude yields in positivity as we often overlook the simple pleasures, privileges and advantages we have been gifted within this lifetime.

Seek to understand, not to criticize.

People will cover up their truth with words in hopes that who they really are or what they really think may be concealed. Be careful what you believe, not everything is to be taken at face value, not everything that is vocalized is the truth so do not treat it as such automatically. Discern and investigate.

4 RELIVING, RELEASE AND RELIEF

Nature Rehab

I wobbled over the stones to reach the centre of the
island, the island in me.
I exhaled to release…breathe, breathe, breath…
The waves hit the shore and washed over the faces of
the rocks closet to it.
A few sprinkles wet my arms and alerted me to it's chill
Goosebumps….
I peered out over the oceans waves, they glistened..
The rhythm of the waves coming in readjusted the
internal rhythm in my body..
Anxiety escaped me…
In that moment, I was present
In that moment I was free
Cleanse me….cleanse me…
Eyes closed, no worry in the world
Fresh water, fresh air, thriving plants, swooping birds
Refreshed, new energy
Watery….water me…
Cleansed, I am free.

Don't let the hurt control you, let it come and go, in waves.

You're broken... I can't fix you, you have to fix yourself.

What you don't resolve, can't evolve.

I have emotions, I just don't let them drown me.

The best pay back is staying in your peace, levelling up and allowing those who want to see you fall instead see you succeed . Leave Karma to do it's work.

Relinquish control of people and situations that can not be controlled. Focus on changing only what is in your power to change. If you can't change it or tolerate it, leave it.

On the other side of pain….is peace. Internal peace.

You can not heal what you continue to conceal.

A wound needs to be treated and tended to or it will become infected. An emotional or spiritual wound works the same way. When you have an experience where you've felt negative emotions or have experienced trauma, if you try to bury it instead of facing it and working through releasing the hurt, you will only end up infecting your daily life subconsciously; without even realizing it. It becomes second nature. What is not resolved will resurface.

When we develop toxic habits of coping, it's because there is unpacked emotional and spiritual baggage that was never resolved. We tend to carry it along with us daily and just find a way to cope by way of distractions and temporary fixes to escape. Distractions and the escapes come to an end and reality hits, now what? It becomes a never ending cycle of medicating the wound without ever curing it. To cure the wound, you have to care for it by opening it up and exposing it to yourself if nobody else. There will be fear of pain or what will surface when the wound is opened or reopened however pain precedes progress.

The longer you wait to unpack baggage, the harder it becomes to do so. Confront a situation in the best way that you know how, as soon as possible before it becomes an infected wound.

Anything and everything is up to personal interpretation. We often tend to be offended by our own perception of what we believe someone said. Release the tendency to be affected by everything you don't like. Release what doesn't apply.

The greatest learning is in challenging what we think we already know, unlearning previously conceived notions and ideas that were based in fear and ignorance. We must instead develop our own perceptions and beliefs about life through experience and observation.

If a thought or idea does not gel with you or produces confusion, explore it, unpack it, then come to a conclusion based on what you know after seeking information about it.

Try to be open as everything we believe is not necessarily the truth. Bad habits, norms and behaviours are passed on generationally through family and societal connections.

When the abundance is ready to come, it comes pouring in. You almost can't believe it but believe it; it's meant for you, embrace it, receive the gifts you've been awaiting without apprehension. You are worthy of it. The unseen good pays off whether the development of those gifts are known to the external world or not. Many things occur outside of our awareness that we are not privy to, regardless of if you believe in God, Gods, Karma, the universe, science, a combination of various views or ideologies or nothing at all.

There are workings at play beyond the scope of our understanding or expertise, we tend to be able to consume and soak up negativity a little too easily. Focus that energy on the positive and your life transforms, it will begin to advance in ways that you did not even know were possible.

Everything starts with the energy in our minds, we then power our thoughts in order to propel them forward. Feed only the thoughts you want to prosper. It's easier said than done but once you begin practicing it regularly, it will start to become the natural response and mindset, there will then be less room for negativity to seep in.

The greatest gift we can give to anyone around us is making a conscious effort to heal our own trauma.

Once you focus on improving yourself and your own circumstances instead of forcing change on others, naturally others will change. Your change becomes a catalyst that influences changes in others at their own will.

Release the idea that you need to hide who you really are in order to be accepted. Those who genuinely love and appreciate you will stay, imperfections and all. The masks will only attract falsehood and prevent true alignment with unconditional love; both from yourself to yourself and from others. Accept yourself in totality so that others may follow suit. Flaws and all.

Everyone judges to some extent. To make a judgment is to reach a conclusion after assessing a person, thing or situation. The danger is that not all judgements are correct.

However, if you never judge, how do you ever make a decision on whether you want to befriend someone or not, whether they are healthy company for you, whether you should enter or stay away from a specific situation?

If you accept every single thing in life that comes to you or by you, I also hope that you don't complain about all of the negative things that happen to you or about the negative people you keep around you.

We are the creators of our lives, we may not be able to control everything but we can control ourselves and what we allow or tolerate around us.

Sacrifice is required to achieve success at some step of the way, often times it's temporary, it won't be forever. Whether it be your time, energy, social life, at the cost of sleep sometimes (very unfortunate), there will be depletion in some area in order to attain great increase in another. Adjust accordingly. Keep going.

.

Cry and cry and cry again as much as you need to,
Feel your emotions, look them in the eye,
Until you navigate through and understand them
And then the ache will be no more.

It can take a lot of time and energy however your mental state of mind and spirituality is worth it. Emotion is human, pain is inevitable, but you can always choose to move forward. Make a conscious effort to face your demons and resolve them until they are no more. Call them out by their names. If you can perceive a behavior or thought process as problematic, call it out or have it identified, you can then find solutions to resolving it. Where there's a will, there's a way.

Demons can be manifested through various bad habits, behavior's and negative thought processes. Past pain and resentment or animosity, unhealthy addictions, bondages of the mind which cause one to constantly act out lustfully and/or in violent or excessive ways to your own detriment are examples of how demonic or bad energy manifests itself.

1) Identify the demons or negativities that you want to destroy or remove from your life because they are keeping you back from the life you desire to live.

2) Go deep and analyze or review when the "demons" took control of your life and you became a servant to them. It is important to reflect on the source of the toxic habits and negative thought processes that can consume you in order to rid yourself from them. The development of demons occur on a subconscious level.

3) Take the initiative to be active in your own healing. Replace bad thoughts with happy ones. Begin exercising or taking yoga. Look into taking counselling sessions. Forgive yourself and let go of resentment, be present in the moment and make a choice to execute actions that will improve your quality of life day by day from this point forward.

ABOUT THE AUTHOR

Candace Shepherd is a writer who is passionate about serving and assisting in the betterment of mankind. She believes in the protection of the vulnerable, the inner workings of the mind and the energy of the spirit. Candace graduated with an Honours Bachelor of Arts in Psychology and a Law of Social Thought Certificate. Candace is the mother of one son who she gave birth to when she was only 17 years of age. She finds internal strength and power in accomplishing her goals in the face of adversity. Born to a Bajan father and a Guyanese mother, she is the youngest of 5 children; two sisters and two brothers. In her spare time, she enjoys meditating, reading, dancing, listening to the sounds of reggae, dancehall, soca, r&b, soul and hip-hop. Candace aspires to be a Mid-Wife, Counsellor and Mentor in hopes of healing and helping humanity.

Order 2000 161 425

29 July.

Printed in Great Britain
by Amazon